The Moon

Contents

What Is the Moon?

The moon is a big ball of rock
that travels around Earth.
It is much closer to Earth
than planets or stars,
but it is still far away.

The moon can be seen
from Earth on most nights
and sometimes in the day.

The moon is not a planet.
Planets travel around the sun.
Moons travel around planets.
Some planets have many moons,
but Earth has only one.

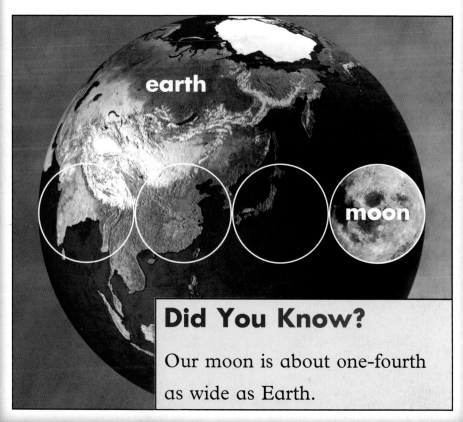

earth

moon

Did You Know?

Our moon is about one-fourth
as wide as Earth.

The moon's path around Earth
is called an orbit.
The moon's orbit is
in the shape
of an oval.

Did You Know?

It takes about a month
for the moon to orbit
Earth once. The
distance between Earth
and the moon changes
during each month.

The moon appears to change size as it moves in the sky.

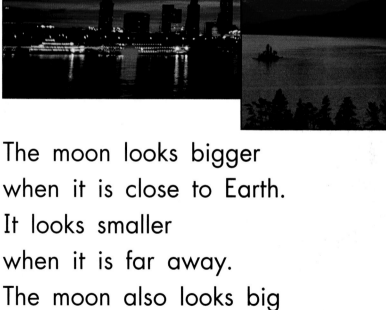

The moon looks bigger
when it is close to Earth.
It looks smaller
when it is far away.
The moon also looks big
when it is low in the sky.

high tide

low tide

Did You Know?

The water in Earth's oceans rises and falls twice each day. These movements are called tides. Tides are caused by the sun and the moon.

Light from the Moon

The moon does not make
its own light.
The moon looks bright
because it reflects the light
from the sun.

The sun's rays light up
the moon.

The moon always keeps
the same shape.
But it looks like
it changes shape
when parts of it are
hidden in darkness.
Sometimes it looks
like a full circle.
Sometimes it can't
be seen at all.

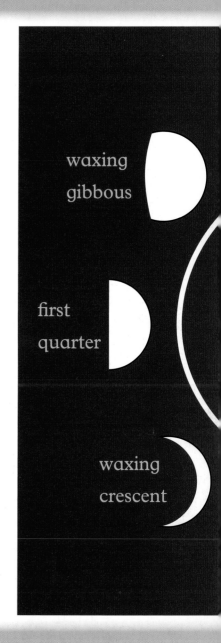

waxing
gibbous

first
quarter

waxing
crescent

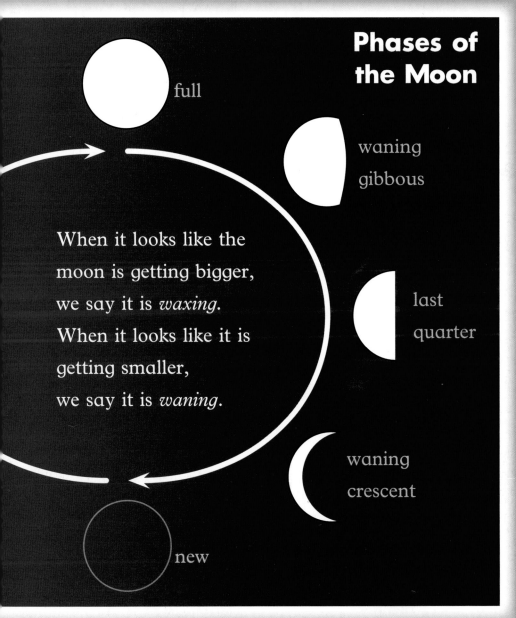

full

waning
gibbous

When it looks like the
moon is getting bigger,
we say it is *waxing*.
When it looks like it is
getting smaller,
we say it is *waning*.

last
quarter

waning
crescent

new

9

On the Moon

The moon has
mountains, plains, and craters.
Most craters are holes
made by rocks
that hit the moon.
The moon does not have air
or weather.
Plants and animals
cannot live on the moon.

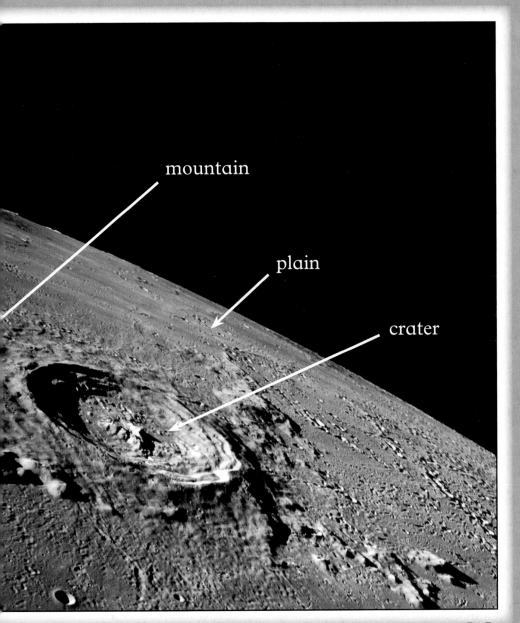

mountain

plain

crater

Did You Know?

There is no noise on the moon because there is no air to carry sound waves.

If you were on the moon, you would need to talk with your hands.

Earth's sky looks blue because of the air around Earth. The moon's sky is always dark because there is no air there.

People on the Moon

People have landed on the moon
to study it.
The first person walked
on the moon in 1969.

Did You Know?

When astronauts travel to the moon, they carry their own air supply to keep them alive.

The Apollo missions were the
first to land people on the moon.

People weigh less on the moon than they do on Earth.

Astronauts need to get used to walking on the moon because they are lighter there.

Will We Live on the Moon?

Many years from now,
people may live on the moon.
We may use the moon as a base
to study planets and stars.
Would you like to live on the moon
someday?

This shows what a moon base might look like.

15

Index